Contents

Introduction

Welcome to *Music Theory in Practice Model Answers*, Grade 3. These answers are a useful resource to help you prepare for ABRSM Theory of Music exams. This book is designed to be used alongside the revised *Music Theory in Practice* workbook (published 2008).

All the answers in this book would receive full marks in an exam. Accepted options are included for cases where an answer may be expressed in more than one way. For composition-style questions, a model answer is provided as an example of good practice.

Using these answers

- Answers are given in the same order and, where possible, in the same layout as in the corresponding *Music Theory in Practice* workbook. This makes it easy to match the answers to the questions.
- Where it is necessary to show the answer on a stave, the original stave is printed in grey with the answer shown in black, for example:

- Alternative answers are separated by an oblique stroke (/) or by *or*, for example:

B / B♮ / B natural

- Answers that require the candidate to write out a scale or chord have been shown at one octave only. Reasonable alternatives at different octaves can also receive full marks.

First published in 2009 by ABRSM (Publishing) Ltd, a wholly owned subsidiary of ABRSM
Reprinted in 2009, 2011, 2012, 2014, 2016, 2018

© 2009 by The Associated Board of the Royal Schools of Music

Typeset by Barnes Music Engraving Ltd
Cover by Okvik Design
Inside design by Vermillion
Printed in England by Caligraving Ltd, Thetford, Norfolk,
on materials from sustainable sources

Exercise 1 ✔

A ♩ lasts as long as 8 ♬

A ♪ lasts as long as 4 ♬

A 𝅝 lasts as long as 32 ♬

A ♪. lasts as long as 6 ♬

A 𝅗𝅥. lasts as long as 24 ♬

A ♩. lasts as long as 12 ♬

Exercise 2 ✔

Exercise 3 ✔

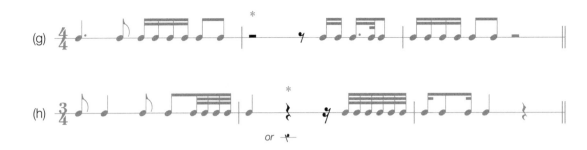

Major keys with four sharps or flats

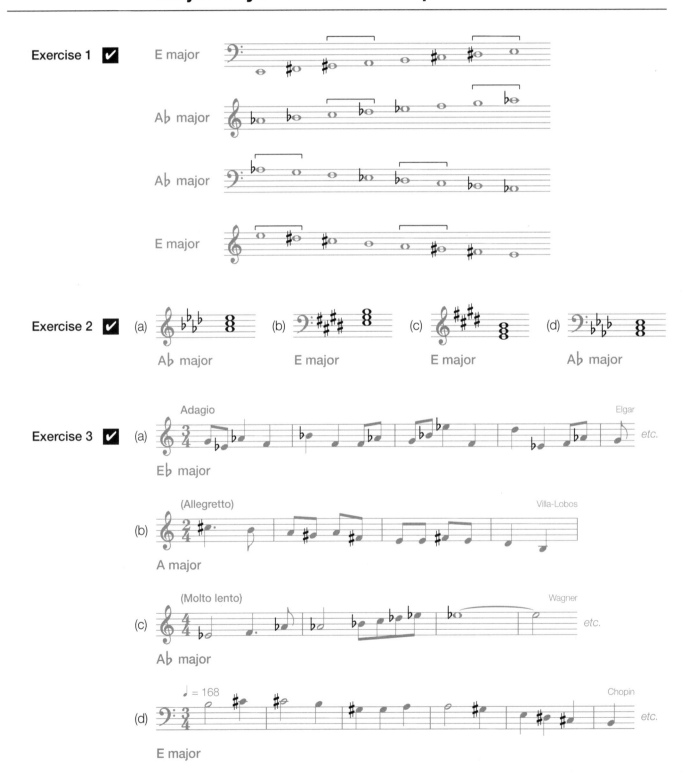

Exercise 1 ✔ E major

Ab major

Ab major

E major

Exercise 2 ✔ (a) Ab major (b) E major (c) E major (d) Ab major

Exercise 3 ✔ (a) Adagio — Elgar — Eb major etc.

(b) (Allegretto) — Villa-Lobos — A major

(c) (Molto lento) — Wagner — Ab major etc.

(d) ♩ = 168 — Chopin — E major etc.

Beyond two ledger lines

Transposition

Exercise 1 ☑ (a)

(b)

Exercise 2 ☑ (a)

Andante maestoso

(b)

(Andante)

(c)

Compound time

Exercise 1 ☑

$\frac{6}{8}$	means	2	beats in a bar, and the beats are	**dotted crotchets (dotted quarter notes)**
$\frac{3}{4}$	means	3	beats in a bar, and the beats are	**crotchets (quarter notes)**
$\frac{9}{8}$	means	3	beats in a bar, and the beats are	**dotted crotchets (dotted quarter notes)**
$\frac{4}{4}$	means	4	beats in a bar, and the beats are	**crotchets (quarter notes)**
$\frac{12}{8}$	means	4	beats in a bar, and the beats are	**dotted crotchets (dotted quarter notes)**

Exercise 2 ☑

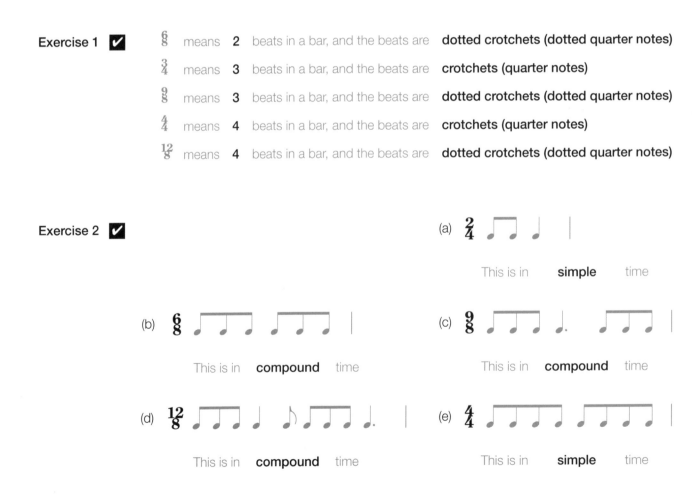

(a) $\frac{2}{4}$

This is in **simple** time

(b) $\frac{6}{8}$

This is in **compound** time

(c) $\frac{9}{8}$

This is in **compound** time

(d) $\frac{12}{8}$

This is in **compound** time

(e) $\frac{4}{4}$

This is in **simple** time

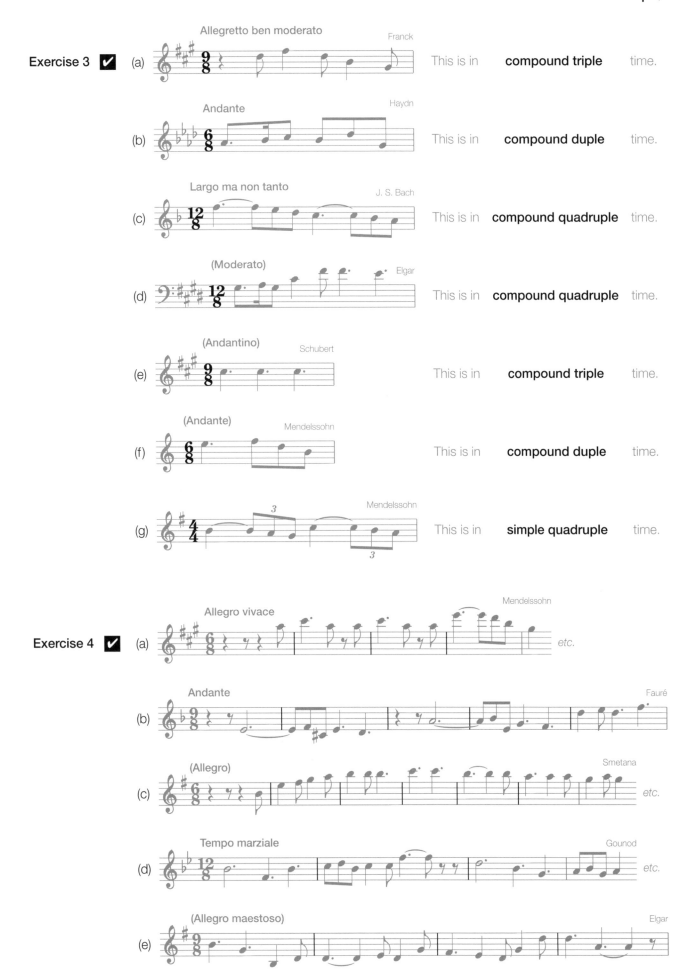

Exercise 3 ✔ (a) *Allegretto ben moderato* — Franck — This is in **compound triple** time.

(b) *Andante* — Haydn — This is in **compound duple** time.

(c) *Largo ma non tanto* — J. S. Bach — This is in **compound quadruple** time.

(d) *(Moderato)* — Elgar — This is in **compound quadruple** time.

(e) *(Andantino)* — Schubert — This is in **compound triple** time.

(f) *(Andante)* — Mendelssohn — This is in **compound duple** time.

(g) Mendelssohn — This is in **simple quadruple** time.

Exercise 4 ✔ (a) *Allegro vivace* — Mendelssohn — *etc.*

(b) *Andante* — Fauré

(c) *(Allegro)* — Smetana — *etc.*

(d) *Tempo marziale* — Gounod — *etc.*

(e) *(Allegro maestoso)* — Elgar

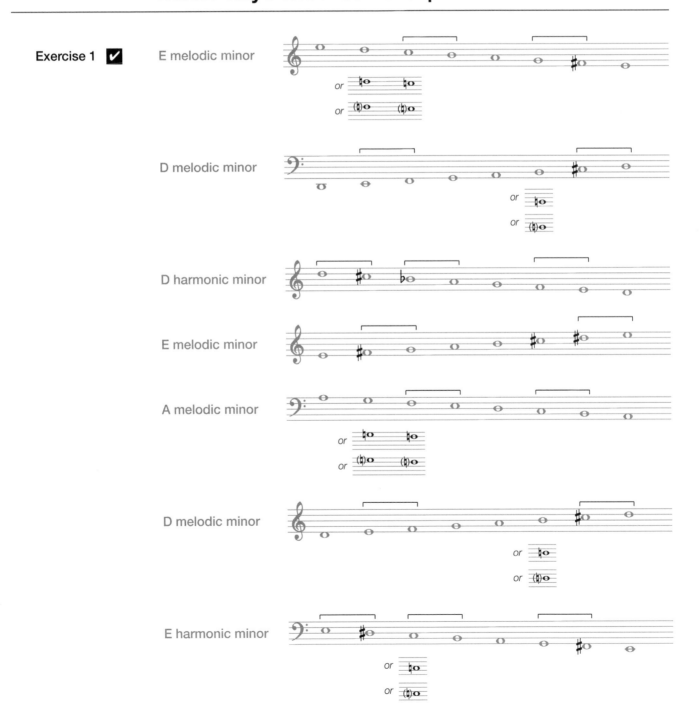

Minor keys with four sharps or flats

Exercise 1 ✔

E melodic minor

D melodic minor

D harmonic minor

E melodic minor

A melodic minor

D melodic minor

E harmonic minor

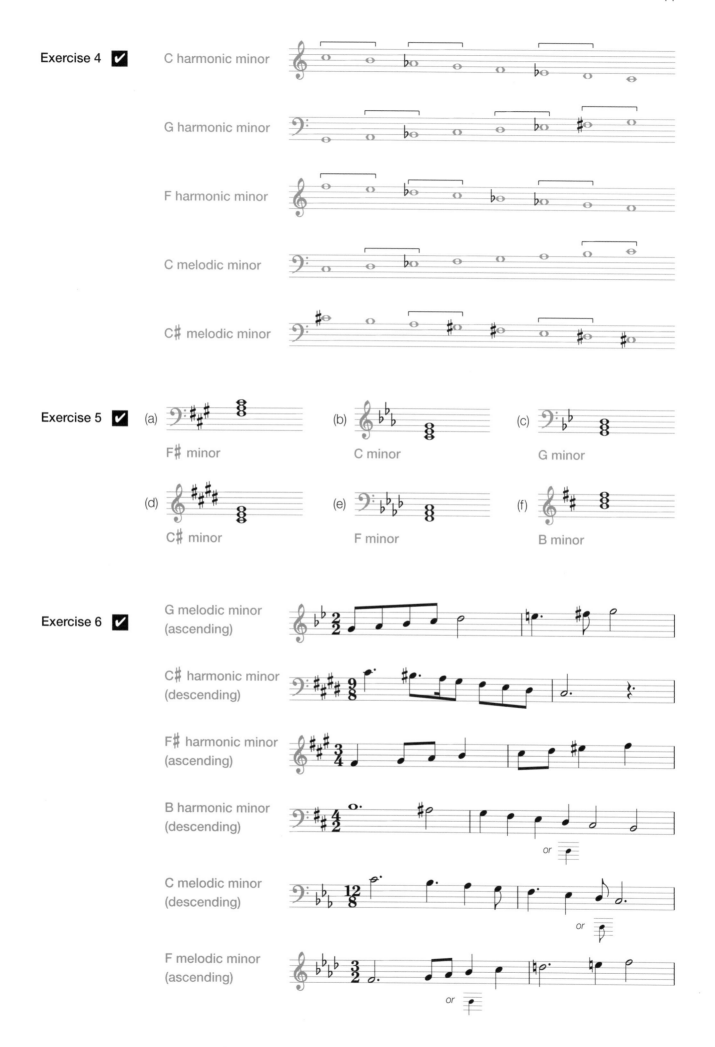

Grouping notes and rests in compound time

Exercise 1 ✔

Scales and key signatures (further practice)

Exercise 1 ✔

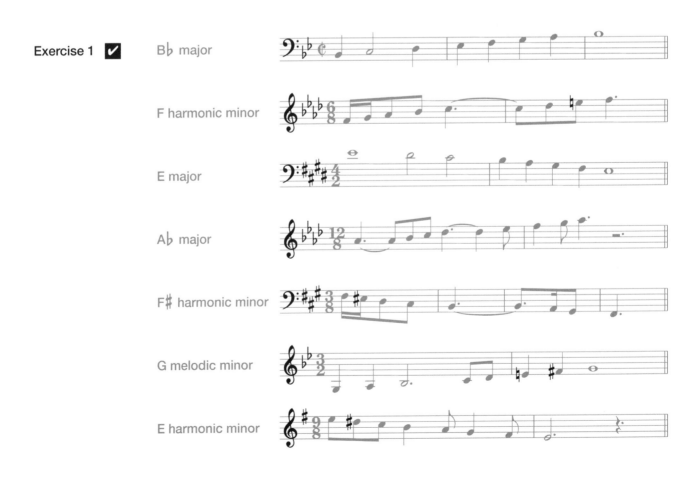

Exercise 2 ✔

Four-bar rhythms

Exercise 1 ✔ There are many ways of completing this exercise. The specimen answers that follow provide examples of good practice.

Exercise 2 ✔ There are many ways of completing this exercise. The specimen answers that follow provide examples of good practice.

Intervals

Exercise 1 ✔

	perfect 4th	major 3rd	major 7th	perfect 4th
minor 6th	major 7th	perfect 8th / 8ve	minor 6th	major 2nd
major 6th	major 2nd	major 6th	major 6th	major 7th
minor 7th	major 6th	perfect 5th	perfect 5th	major 7th
minor 7th	perfect 4th	perfect 5th	minor 3rd	major 2nd

Exercise 2 ✔ (a)   1   **perfect 5th**   2   **major 6th**

(b)   1   **minor 3rd**   2   **perfect 4th**

(c)   1   **minor 6th**   2   **perfect 4th**   3   **minor 3rd**

(d)   1   **minor 6th**   2   **perfect 4th**   3   **perfect 8th / 8ve**   4   **perfect 5th**

Simple phrase structure

Exercise 1 ☑ (a)

General exercises

Exercise 1 ✔

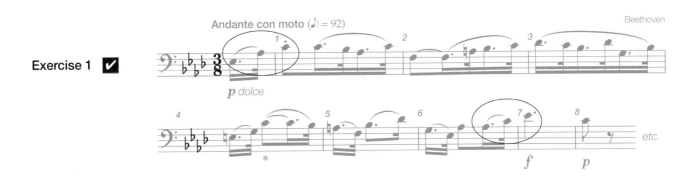

(a) The answer is provided in the opening bar and bar 4 in the extract reproduced above.

(b) The answer is provided in the opening bar in the extract reproduced above.

(c) **E♮ / E flat** in bar **7**

(d) Bar **2** and bar **4**

(e) **they are an octave apart / both notes are E♭ / E flat**

(f) (i) **at a walking pace with movement / medium speed with movement**
     (ii) **92 quaver (eighth-note) beats in a minute**
     (iii) **sweet / soft / sweetly**

(g) **major 3rd**

(h) There are two answers circled in the extract reproduced above: the opening three notes; bars 6–7.

(i)

Exercise 2 ✔   (a)   **slow / stately / slow and stately**

(b)   **C minor**

(c)   **E♭ major**

(d)

simple	compound	duple	triple	quadruple
✔	☐	☐	✔	☐

(e)   Bar **2** and bar **3**

(f)   (i)   **perfect 5th**
       (ii)   **minor 6th**

(g)

(h)   **7**

(i)   **they all belong to the tonic triad of C minor**

(j)   **A♭ / A flat** in bars **7** and **8**

(k)

Exercise 3 ✔   (a)

(b)   **simple triple**

(c)   **D minor**

(d)

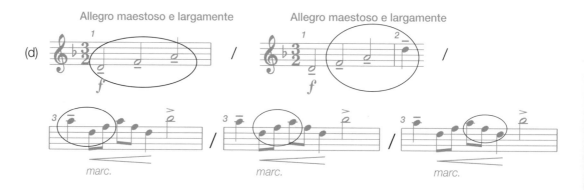

(e) **B♮ / B flat** in bar **3**

(f) **it is the same in each bar**

(g)   (i)   **fast majestic and broadly**
       (ii)   **accented / emphatic / with emphasis**
       (iii) **slight pressure / emphasis**
       (iv)   **accent**
       (v)   **tie these notes so that the sound lasts for 2 full beats / 2 minims (half notes)**

(h)

Exercise 4 ✔ (a) **A minor**

(b)

(c)   simple   compound   duple   triple   quadruple
         ☐   ✔   ✔   ☐   ☐

(d)   (i)   **perfect 4th**
       (ii)   **minor 3rd**

(e)   (i)   **at a walking pace / medium speed**
       (ii)   **quiet / soft**

(f) **5th**

(g) **first note of bar 3**

(h) **they indicate phrase marks**

(i) **they have the same rhythm**

(j)

Acknowledgements

Page 4: Elgar, *'Enigma' Variations* ('Nimrod')
© Copyright 1899 Novello & Co. Ltd
All rights reserved. Reproduced for sale in France, Spain, Italy and Mexico by permission of Novello & Co. Ltd.

Page 4: Villa-Lobos, *Guia Pratico* Album 8 ('Carambola')
© Copyright 1948 (renewed) Music Sales Corporation (ASCAP).
Chester Music Ltd trading as Campbell Connelly & Co.
All rights reserved. International copyright secured.
Used by permission of Chester Music Ltd trading as Campbell Connelly & Co.

Page 5: Walford Davies, *R.A.F. March Past*
© Copyright 1921 Boosey & Hawkes Music Publishers Ltd
Reproduced by permission.

Page 5: Sibelius, *Valse Triste*
© Breitkopf & Härtel, Wiesbaden

Page 7: Elgar, Cello Concerto (1st mvt)
© Copyright 1919 Novello & Co. Ltd
All rights reserved. Reproduced for sale in France, Spain, Italy and Mexico by permission of Novello & Co. Ltd.

Page 7: Elgar, Organ Sonata, Op. 28 (1st mvt)
© Copyright 1908 Breitkopf & Härtel, Wiesbaden for France, Spain and Mexico

Page 16: Oscar Straus, 'Love's Roundabout'
© Copyright 1950 Editions Choudens/Premiere Music Group.
Chester Music Ltd trading as Campbell Connelly & Co.
All rights reserved. International copyright secured.
Used by permission of Chester Music Ltd trading as Campbell Connelly & Co.

Page 16: Walford Davies, *Solemn Melody*
© Copyright 1910 Novello & Co. Ltd.
All rights reserved. International copyright secured. Used by permission.

Page 18: Purcell/Britten, Theme from *Young Person's Guide to the Orchestra*
© Copyright 1947 Hawkes & Son (London) Ltd
Reproduced by permission of Boosey & Hawkes Music Publishers Ltd.